Marlowe R. Scott

A PURPOSE FOR EVERYTHING UNDER THE SUN

Marlowe R. Scott

Pearly Gates Publishing, LLC, Houston, Texas (USA)

Wings: A Purpose for Everything Under the Sun

Wings:
A Purpose for Everything Under the Sun

Copyright © 2021
Marlowe R. Scott

All Right Reserved.
No portion of this publication may be reproduced, stored in an electronic system, or transmitted in any form or by any means (electronic, mechanical, photocopy, recording, or otherwise) without written permission from the author or publisher. Brief quotations may be used in literary reviews.

Print ISBN 13: 978-1-948853-21-7
Digital ISBN 13: 978-1-948853-22-4
Library of Congress Control Number: 2021902629

Scripture references are taken from the King James Version (KJV) of the Holy Bible and used with permission via Zondervan at Biblegateway.com. Public Domain.

For information and bulk ordering, contact:
Pearly Gates Publishing, LLC
Angela Edwards, CEO
P.O. Box 62287
Houston, TX 77205
BestSeller@PearlyGatesPublishing.com

Dedication

This book is dedicated to one of the most unselfish, dedicated, and supportive couples I know:

Mr. Joseph Butler
&
Mrs. Rosalee Butler.

I desire to show appreciation for their endless activities in servitude to others in my own humble way. Each of them is truly a *"Doer of God's Word."*

Biography of Mr. Joseph Butler

Joseph Butler is a U.S. Air Force Vietnam Veteran. Following his military duty, he returned home and was hired as the first African-American police officer in Queen Anne's County, Maryland. Upon relocating to New Jersey, Joseph began a 30-year career with the New Jersey Department of Corrections. During his tenure, he rose through the ranks and held positions as an Officer, Internal Affairs Investigator, Assistant Superintendent, Associate Administrator, Administrator (Warden), and Director of Operations.

Joseph joined Tabernacle Baptist Church in Burlington, New Jersey, in 1989. In addition to attending Sunday services, Sunday School, and Bible Study, he served in many ministries, including the Soup Kitchen, Pantry, Holiday Baskets, Church Security, Church Auditor, and Pastor Input Team.

Joseph also gave back to his community through his roles as Vice-Chairman of the Zoning Board and Chairman of the Board of Trustees for New Jersey Adult Prisons. A lifelong supporter of his high school alumni association, he was a major contributor to the restoration of the Kennard High School African-American Cultural Heritage Center and Museum in Centerville, Maryland.

In addition to all his church and community activities, Joseph enjoys spending time with his family and friends, traveling, fishing, watching football, and being an avid lighthouse collector. Joseph has been married to his wife, Rosalee, for 50 years. From their union, they have one daughter, Taneisa.

Biography of Mrs. Rosalee Butler

Rosalee Butler is a retired Physical Education and Health teacher. A graduate of the University of Maryland Eastern Shore, she taught in the public school system in Trenton, New Jersey, for 31 years.

In 1989, Rosalee joined Tabernacle Baptist Church in Burlington, New Jersey. To increase her knowledge of God's Word and to strive to be a "Doer of His Words," Rosalee attends daily prayer, Bible classes, Wednesday Word with Pastor Cory, and Sunday worship services.

Rosalee has been an active member of various church ministries. To her credit and God's glory, she has held the following positions: Vice President, Treasurer, and Financial Secretary of QUEST; Coordinator of the Soup Kitchen; Thanksgiving and Christmas Food Baskets Distribution; and President,

Treasurer, and Financial Secretary of the Senior Usher Board. She has faithfully served on the Senior Usher Board for 31 years.

Always willingly and unselfishly, Rosalee supports other service organizations by providing food, clothing, shoes, and financial support by sponsoring children in Nicaragua, Haiti, and Africa for the past 50 years. Her giving has also provided funding for the construction of new homes for families in Jamaica and Nicaragua. Along with her husband, she was also recognized as a major contributor to the restoration of the Kennard High School African-American Cultural Heritage Center and Museum in Centerville, Maryland.

Rosalee and her husband, Joseph, celebrated 50 years of marriage in 2020. They are blessed with a daughter, Taneisa.

Rosalee's favorite Bible verse is Philippians 4:13:

"I can do all things through CHRIST who strengthens me."

Acknowledgments

I must first and always give thanks and praises to my God, my Lord and Savior Jesus Christ, and the blessings of the Holy Spirit. The many inspirations and gifts given to me are humbling. The unconditional love, protection, lessons, inspirations, and messages bestowed upon me to share with others have been more than awesome as I continue my earthly journey. **PRAISES** and **HALLELUJAH!**

Secondly, to my award-winning daughter, Angela R. Edwards—the CEO, Publisher, and Chief Editorial Director of Pearly Gates Publishing, LLC of Houston, Texas. Her talents and gifts are forever growing, as she also serves and encourages others on her literary journey. I am proud to say that every book Pearly Gates Publishing publishes in her growing business is truly First Class!

Preface

Wings: A Purpose for Everything Under the Sun stems from several aspects of my personal experiences related to reading and studying the Holy Scriptures. Many verses, stories, and parables throughout the Bible are based on Creation. The trees, waters, animals, and fowls of the air were often used as examples so that people in early biblical times could understand God's prophets and other messages for His children. Even Jesus Christ used earthly elements and the animals God created in His parables. Today, those parables are provided to us as clear examples for help understanding the intended messages.

As one who is familiar with earth's creation story, I was prompted to recall a pet white leghorn hen and how, in the Book of Ecclesiastes, there is "a time and purpose for everything under the sun." The chicken showed me—and scripture confirmed—although she could fly, her wings were created with the ability to be the perfect covering when trouble or danger was near, and she could protect her chicks under her wings.

Introduction

Included on the pages of this book are scriptures and examples about birds, as well as an original Spirit-inspired poem written by the author. The narrative uses other birds/fowl, but the primary focus is on the chicken's wings to illustrate the following points:

- ❖ God has and continues to protect us.
- ❖ There are places to "run" when danger arises in our lives.
- ❖ God can and does use simple things to confound the wise (as found in 1 Corinthians 1:25): "Because the foolishness of God is wiser than man; and the weakness of God is stronger than men."

Beginning with the Holy Scripture's Book of Genesis, there are histories of humankind and the creation of Heaven and Earth, including examples of how the land, seas, plants, and animals of every kind were created. Among those animals were birds and fowl, with each species having wings. The wings' purposes may be to fly, while others may instead have strong legs for running.

A few birds recorded explicitly in scripture are the **Swift, Thrush, Owl, Raven, Hawk,** and **Sparrow**. Later in this book, there are listed scriptures referencing the **Hen** and her chicks.

Table of Contents

DEDICATION	VI
BIOGRAPHY OF MR. JOSEPH BUTLER	VII
BIOGRAPHY OF MRS. ROSALEE BUTLER	IX
ACKNOWLEDGMENTS	XII
PREFACE	XIII
INTRODUCTION	XV
CHAPTER ONE: "BE DUCKS"	1
CHAPTER TWO: GOD'S PROTECTIVE WINGS	5
A POEM: WINGS: A PURPOSE FOR EVERYTHING UNDER THE SUN	8
CHAPTER THREE: THE MOTHER HEN'S PROTECTIVE WINGS	11
CHAPTER FOUR: THREE PARTS IN ONE	15
CHAPTER FIVE: "HOLY BIRD!"	18
CHAPTER SIX: THE DAY OF EPIPHANY	20
CLOSING PRAYER	23
BIRDS OF A FEATHER WORD FIND	24
POINTS TO PONDER: JOURNALING PAGES	25
WORD FIND SOLUTION	33
ABOUT THE AUTHOR	34

Marlowe R. Scott

"You were born with potential. You were born with goodness and trust. You were born with ideals and dreams. You were born with greatness. You were born with wings. You are not meant for crawling, so don't. You have wings. Learn to use them and fly."

~ Rumi ~

(Rumi was born September 30, 1207, in Afghanistan and died December 17, 1273, in Turkey.)

Wings: A Purpose for Everything Under the Sun

Chapter One
"Be Ducks"

Growing up, I played with many animals that had wings, like my caged pet parakeets and canaries. I recall how, during the Summer months, there were fireflies at night which could be caught and placed into a jar to make a play lantern. However, there is a fowl that relates to my growing up as a farm girl in the southern parts of New Jersey.

My closest relationship with a fowl was a pet white leghorn hen I affectionately named "Be Ducks." Do not ask why I chose that name, as I do not have an answer. Regarding the spelling of her name, I am merely guessing what it might have been based on how it sounds phonetically.

"Be Ducks" was the last of chicks my family had raised one year. She became my pet because she allowed me to feed her and, eventually, let me pet, pick her up, and rub under her wings. She really enjoyed that! As a hen, she regularly laid eggs. Many were double-yolked! How did I know, you ask? Well, when she would perch on the inside wooden frame on which the shed was built, some of her eggs would fall to the floor and break open—exposing two yolks.

What a waste…but that was "Be Ducks"!

As my pet, she would follow me around in the yard, clucking away! She also came when I called out to her or when she wanted special "petting time." The unique habit she developed was to squat down, let me pick her up, and rub under her wings (as stated before).

By this point, you might be wondering, *"What in the world does "Be Ducks" have to do with an inspirational book?"* Be ever-mindful that I started with scripture and God's Creation. As you, too, study the scriptures, you will find birds mentioned throughout, such as the familiar eagle.

But wait! The hen is there, too! Thus, I share the following passage of scriptures with you (note their likenesses):

"*O Jerusalem, Jerusalem, thou that killest the prophets, and stonest them which are sent unto thee; how often would I have gathered thy children together, even as a **hen gathereth her chickens under her wings**, and ye would not!*" (Matthew 23:27, emphasis added)

NOTE: *Luke 13:34 has very similar wording.*

Wings: A Purpose for Everything Under the Sun

Chapter Two
God's Protective Wings

The Old Testament Book of Psalms has numerous beautiful words to guide us. The following verse is used as a reference for this chapter:

"He shall cover thee with His feathers, and under His wings shall thou trust; His truth shall be thy shield and bucker" (Psalm 91:4).

In Sunday School classes, Bible studies, and sermons over the years, verses from Psalm 91 have been taught many times. There are numerous spiritual messages throughout it. The referenced fourth verse speaks of God's feathers, under His wings of trust, and having a shield and buckler.

In biblical times, the shield was a common war protector made of wood that was bound together with leather, reeds, or perhaps animal hides. There were different shapes and used for years, although bulky.

The buckler was similar to a shield but smaller and lighter. It might have been used for personal defense rather than war.

To me, it means that whether we have to fight alone or in a war, God will always cover and protect us. **AMEN?** *YES!* **AMEN!!!**

A Poem
Wings: A Purpose for Everything Under the Sun

Marlowe R. Scott © 2021

God, when creating our Earth, took love and care to put in place

Everything we would need, including birds and fowl,

With beautiful feathers of countless hues.

Some are bright yellow, white, and even blue.

These feathers are definitely useful,

As the birds fly and strut about around me and you.

Scriptures share a clear example

Of the hen using her wings and feathers

As protection of her little chicks.

The message was to show God's rebellious people

That the hen knew better than they did,

Because they had chosen and turned to worldly ways.

Those who had disobeyed God were in trouble.

They had turned away and forgotten their God.

The simple message illustrated by a hen

Makes a significant statement,

And scripture teaches a different plan

That resonates truths to my soul and memories.

I have witnessed a hen calling and gathering her chicks,

Then tucking them in until completely covered.

The chicks rested there until a danger passed or

Each night to gather in under her warm wings to soundly sleep.

Yes, I know as the scriptures illustrate

The hen is wiser than some of mankind.

The next time you see a bird or feather,

Maybe you will reflect on this short poem

And remember to FIRST seek GOD in prayer.

GOD, JESUS CHRIST, and THE HOLY SPIRIT

Are always available to listen and comfort

Any burden, danger, sadness and more we must bear.

Another valuable message is offered —

It is to use our "human wings"

Which are our arms and hands, to HELP, LOVE,

ENCOURAGE, and SHARE with our fellow man;

Genuinely loving our neighbor as our ourselves

By following Our Savior Jesus Christ's Command!

Chapter Three
The Mother Hen's Protective Wings

Referring back to the New Testament examples of the hen as found in the Books of Matthew and Luke, both share her as spreading her wings to protect her chicks. Both instances follow after God laments after His people—Israel—rejected the prophets sent to them. A partial cause of the rejection may have been that the Israelites were actually foreigners while in Jerusalem. Some had intermingled and married the people there.

However (and whenever God's chosen people disobeyed), He had a way to illustrate truth to them: the **HEN**! Jesus also used nature a lot in His stories, examples, and parables. There most likely were chickens living around the area, even in the cities and marketplaces being sold for food.

With the noises, children playing, and people trying to catch a chicken for food, many a mother hen used the protective wings God gave her to gather her chicks under her. It is amazing how many little yellow chicks I have seen go under a hen's wings. They are trained early by their mother hen to come when called and go under her wings for protection or to bed down for the night.

What a loving example God's Word provides! He certainly protects us in different ways, including:

- ❖ Through a sermon spoken just in time to suit your needs/problems at a particular time.
- ❖ Being alert to avoid an accident.
- ❖ Providing unexpected help when you felt completely helpless.
- ❖ Inner feeling to help/visit/call someone who needs assistance or just to hear your voice.
- ❖ Recalling a past experience so you won't do it again when tempted or using that experience to help someone overcome the issue.

So, you see, we are protected from dangers both seen and unseen!

Furthermore, we are protected from the rains and winds under those wing examples during the many "storms" in our lives. We are protected from predators and things trying to get near us, seeking to do harm physically and, especially, **SPIRITUALLY**!

Indeed, we can find contentment and peace under those Spiritual Wings, just as the baby chicks find the same with their mother hen.

Chapter Four
Three Parts in One

When talking about wings—especially chicken wings—it is likely you immediately thought of food. Chicken wings are used as appetizers with dips and sauces, fried, barbequed, baked, and more. The chicken can be made into salads, and cooked in soups and stews, with the broth used as the base for many dishes. Even the feet are used. ***Yes, even the feet!*** (Check on the internet and in cookbooks, should you be inclined to explore.)

Hens are used for the production of eggs in the farm setting. Unlike the chicken coops I was familiar with, I was deeply upset the first time I went to a farm in Virginia and found the chickens being housed in little cages stacked in a large barn. They were not free-roaming and did not know freedom as God intended. Rather, they were there for one purpose: to produce eggs for the market.

To this day, I often reflect on how the egg is a three-part, valuable food product used for breakfast, salads, baking, and other things when separated.

During Youth Fellowship at the Methodist church where I received my years of basic Christian Education, the teacher used an egg to illustrate the three parts of the Trinity!

One egg…three parts in one.

1. **The yolk:** Jesus Christ.
2. **The egg white:** The Holy Spirit.
3. **The shell:** Holding it all together and covering the whole "egg" — God the Father and Creator.

Marlowe R. Scott

Chapter Five
"HOLY BIRD!"

God created the chicken with everything it needed from head to toe, just as He did with other animals.

People around chickens—especially roosters—have been awakened early in the morning by the "cock-a-doodle-doo"! Farmers don't need an alarm clock when there's a rooster or two nearby!

Over the years, the chicken became known as the "Holy Bird" because, at almost every special occasion (i.e., wedding, anniversary, etc.), fried or baked chicken was the main meat dish.

Many a church was built on the sale of chicken (and fish) dinners. I often remember members asking, *"What will be the dinner served?"* when we visited other congregations. Ninety-five percent of the time, the answer was: ***"The Holy Bird"!***

Chapter Six
The Day of Epiphany

In recent years, the United States of America experienced many tragic events over race, sexual preferences, supremacy issues, and numerous other injustices. The following poem was inspired and written on January 7, 2021, concerning the attack on the U.S.A. Capitol in Washington, D.C. on January 6, 2021 (which was also 'The Day of Epiphany' in Christianity).

You are invited to read, contemplate, and somehow use your actions and words to make a difference! The following poem was also shared on Facebook.

> The time has come.
> It's long OVERDUE.
> Say OUT LOUD,
> "JESUS, I love You!
> You taught us the way.
> Now, we must stand and say,
> 'Get behind us, evil Satan;
> You have no place in my day!

Marlowe R. Scott

My keeper is Jesus.

You, devil, have gotten in the way

Of leaders in our country — the USA!

Christians are praying that your

Evilness will be stopped…put away!

Your time is getting shorter,

And your followers are desperately

Causing hate, fear, death, and decay.

GET BEHIND US SATAN!

YOU WILL NOT GET YOUR WAY!!!'"

Jesus Saves Every Day,

As We Continually Obey and Pray!

Closing Prayer

Dear Heavenly Father,

Once again, we praise and thank You for the blessing of writing and sharing Your love with others. May your people's, as well as the communities around the globe, needs be met by others like the awesome couple to whom this book has been dedicated: Joseph and Rosalee Butler.

As we continue the work You have directed us to do, we thank You for the wisdom and strength to keep on keeping on.

Most of all, thank You for the life Your Son Jesus Christ sacrificed for our salvation and the Blessed Holy Spirit, which came to abide within our hearts and souls!

In Jesus' Mighty Name we pray, Amen.

Marlowe R. Scott

Birds of a Feather Word Find

C	F	E	E	I	H	C	W	I	N	G	S	E	T
H	E	E	A	O	S	G	G	E	K	H	C	Y	L
I	A	G	C	N	N	K	K	L	D	C	H	R	H
C	T	K	F	O	W	L	H	F	O	H	O	L	E
K	H	O	K	S	L	R	S	S	V	H	C	L	C
E	E	R	E	N	E	O	C	L	E	K	G	F	O
N	R	Y	R	S	G	E	E	E	S	A	G	E	K
G	S	T	O	K	H	E	I	K	E	S	S	L	R
R	G	E	O	S	O	T	A	I	O	K	K	G	D
K	W	F	S	O	R	H	I	Y	C	H	C	L	G
E	E	A	T	E	N	L	O	I	N	C	U	E	S
A	A	S	E	A	R	L	H	H	S	H	L	L	K
G	L	K	R	E	K	C	F	V	C	E	C	O	K
C	U	S	S	S	H	E	C	Y	O	N	E	S	T

FOWL	EAGLE	CLUCK
FEATHERS	LEGHORN	CHICKS
YOLKS	DOVES	ROOSTER
NEST	WINGS	SAFETY
HEN	CHICKEN	EGGS

Points to Ponder Journaling Pages

1. The quote of Rumi written centuries ago is wise. How did the words touch you?

_____

_____

_____

_____

_____

_____

_____

_____

_____

_____

_____

_____

_____

_____

_____

Marlowe R. Scott

2. A hen might seem like a "foolish" bird, but God did not. In what ways have your views changed about chickens?

_____
_____
_____
_____
_____
_____
_____
_____
_____
_____
_____
_____
_____
_____
_____
_____

Marlowe R. Scott

3. The egg used to explain The Trinity has remained with me for over 60 years. How do you understand and explain The Trinity to others?

_____
_____
_____
_____
_____
_____
_____
_____
_____
_____
_____
_____
_____
_____
_____
_____

4. In what ways have you experienced God's protection covering you?

_____

_____

_____

_____

_____

_____

_____

_____

_____

_____

_____

_____

_____

_____

_____

_____

Marlowe R. Scott

Wings: A Purpose for Everything Under the Sun

Word Find Solution

About the Author

Marlowe R. Scott was born 1944 to the late Carl and Helena Harris. She is the youngest of three and the sole surviving sibling, a mother of three, a grandmother of five, and a great-grandmother of twelve. As a child, Marlowe always loved animals and nature in general. Before attending school, she learned how to read and memorized many of the rhyming stories in Mother Goose books.

With her parents and brothers, Marlowe attended John Wesley Methodist Church in Bridgeton, New Jersey, where she learned hymns, went to Sunday School and Methodist Youth Fellowship, and sang in the Junior Choir. A special memory she has is when, during the Civil Rights Movement of the 1960s, she participated in a nonviolent march from the church to the Cumberland County Courthouse steps in Bridgeton.

Marlowe was taught and developed personal confidence early in her youth. The familiar words of her mother still ring true and are often spoken today by others:

> *"You are no better than anyone else,*
> *and nobody is better than you."*

Teachers enjoyed having her in classes, as she was intelligent, participated, and articulated very well. In 1962, when she was a Senior in Bridgeton High School, she was chosen to be the Lead Speaker in the graduation voice choir, which quoted a portion of Ecclesiastes 3.

Later, as a member of Friendship A.M.E. Church in Browns Mills, New Jersey, Marlowe taught Sunday School, sang in various choirs, ushered, and worked with the Missionaries. She was also the Pastor's Steward to the first woman pastor of the church. Because of her experiences, she was elected Lay President of the Atlantic City District of New Jersey of the 1st Episcopal District of the A.M.E. Church. The Atlantic City District had 31 churches she visited, and she was charged with coordinating events, as well as other religious activities. In February 2020, she received recognition at Tabernacle Baptist Church in Burlington, New Jersey for her inspiring and encouraging literary works.

Marlowe retired from the workforce after 33 years of government civil service. She has found her voice now through writing inspirational books and poetry. She has penned the following Best-Selling books, which are available through Pearly Gates Publishing's website and Amazon:

- ❖ Spiritual Growth: From Milk to Strong Meat
- ❖ Keeping It Real: The Straight and Narrow
- ❖ Believing Without Seeing: The Power of Faith
- ❖ Worth the Journey: The Train Ride to Glory *(A trilogy of the three listed above)*
- ❖ Never Alone: Intimate Times with Jesus
- ❖ Plentiful Harvest: Fertile Ground
- ❖ I AM Cares: His Eyes Are on the Sparrow
- ❖ Abiding is Not Hiding: Safe in His Arms
- ❖ Pentecost: Where the Spirit of God Is
- ❖ Talli's Ancestry Surprise: Beginning the Ancestral Search *(A children's/family book)*

A personal theme Marlowe has adopted for her life is the Serenity Prayer:

"God, grant me the **SERENITY**

to accept the things I cannot change,

the **COURAGE** to change

the things I can,

and the **WISDOM**

to know the difference."

www.ingramcontent.com/pod-product-compliance
Lightning Source LLC
Chambersburg PA
CBHW052126110526
44592CB00013B/1763